How to Avoid *HIPAA* Headaches

Lessons from Avoidable Expensive, Embarassing, and Career-Killing HIPAA Penalties & Data Breaches

MIKE SEMEL

Contents

Foreword.. ix

Myths & Facts about What is Protected by HIPAA............................ 1
Laws, Rules, and other Confusion.. 7
Civil Rights & Real Victims 11
Free and Easy can be Very Expensive & Difficult............................17
Business Associates: Trusted Vendors, or Huge Business Risks?........... 23
Don't be a Slow Learner... a Clock is Ticking (somewhere)................ 33
Data is Worth More than Gold.. 42
I Googled Myself and Found My Medical Records 48
You Lost WHAT??? It was encrypted, RIGHT???..............................54
Will Insurance Save You? Is Insurance an Alternative
    to Investing in Compliance? 60
Regulation Through Litigation.. 64
Why Aren't HIPAA Security Basics No-Brainers? 71
Skilled Nursing & Home Health Care... 80
Should You Do Your Own Security Risk Analysis? 86

Endorsements & Accolades 95
About the Author.. 97

Dedication

For Rose, and my wonderful family, always at my side

For Darren, my first HIPAA teacher

For Jean, my biggest cheerleader

Foreword

What is the better way to understand how speed limits are enforced-reading the traffic laws or knowing someone who was stopped for doing 72 mph in a 55 mph zone on Route 427, and who paid $ 183 in fines and court costs? (Please don't ask me how I know.)

- I've had people tell me they understand HIPAA because they have read the laws.

- I've had people tell me they understand HIPAA because they have read the Privacy, Security, Data Breach Reporting, and HIPAA Omnibus Final rules.

- I've had people tell me they understand HIPAA because they have read the guidance documents and the Frequently Asked Questions on the HIPAA website.

- I've had people tell me they understand HIPAA because they bought a policy manual that sits on their shelf, or filled out a long questionnaire on a website that promises to make HIPAA easy.

- I've had people tell me they understand HIPAA because they went to a conference and heard me speak for 45 minutes outlining some high-level compliance requirements.

They were all wrong. Their misunderstandings far outweighed their knowledge, often with bad results.

You can read the laws, rules, guidance, FAQ, and policies all day long and still not understand what you should and shouldn't do.

But, like the speeding ticket, knowing how the laws are enforced can tell you what you need to know.

Hacking accounts for the largest number of <u>records</u> breached, but **lost unencrypted media and devices** make up the largest <u>number</u> of incidents. You will correctly assume that stolen laptops are common, but it would probably surprise you to see how many breaches have been caused by lost or stolen file servers, desktop computers, portable hard drives, thumb drives, CD's, DVD's, and backup tapes.

While there is an official federal HIPAA enforcement agency, the Office for Civil Rights (OCR), HIPAA is also enforced by state attorneys general. Other agencies enforce data breaches of various types, including those involving medical records. In recent years, the Federal Trade Commission has exercised its authority by claiming a breach is a failure to protect consumers. State insurance commissioners have issued large fines for HIPAA breaches and compliance violations. In some cases, multiple agencies have issued penalties for the same incident.

In a 2013 interview with Modern Healthcare, Leon Rodriguez, the Director of the Office for Civil Rights who ramped up assessing large financial penalties for HIPAA breaches, said the OCR financial penalties are against organizations where the investigations "reveal longstanding and systemic failures to comply with the privacy and security rules."

Financial settlements and fines are just a portion of the actual costs of a data breach. Legal fees, hiring forensic experts, consultants, notification costs, public relations expenses, paying for victims' credit monitoring, settling or losing lawsuits, recovering lost trust, and permanent loss of business are all potential consequences of a breach.

The Ponemon Institute issues an annual 'Cost of a Data Breach' report. The 2016 report listed the cost of a healthcare data breach at $ 401 per lost record. Losing 10,000 records equals $ 4 million. Losing 25,000 records is $ 10 million.

About one third of the cost was to mitigate the breach itself. The other two-thirds were the impact on the business.

Don't believe those numbers?

One of the incidents described in this book started out with a lost laptop and ended up costing the company over $ 600 million. A settlement with a Business Associate for another breach was $ 650,000 for losing 412 records – over $ 1500 per record. A federal HIPAA settlement averaged out to over $ 1 million per patient. A federal fine was calculated at $ 1,000 per day for non-compliance, plus $ 1,000 per patient record.

This is your chance to learn from real incidents, real investigations, real payments, and real misery, so you can avoid suffering a similar fate.

I'm not an attorney, and suggest you direct any questions about your liability, patient notices, Business Associate Agreements, contracts, data use agreements, and legal obligations to a competent healthcare attorney familiar with your organization, federal and state laws, and industry regulations.

I have included several incidents that have not (yet) resulted in federal HIPAA penalties, and some experiences with our own clients where we were able to identify hidden risks and prevent breaches and compliance violations.

Don't think it will ever happen to you? That's what everyone in this book also thought. Please don't become an example for my next book.

I've included some examples of how we helped clients avoid problems, so you can learn from those who asked for our help and did not suffer the embarrassment and expense of a breach.

Want to avoid a data breach? Want to validate that your compliance efforts are working? Not sure if your staff really "has HIPAA handled"?

Visit www.semelconsulting.com and use the Contact link.

Myths & Facts about What is Protected by HIPAA

<u>Who</u> is (and isn't) covered by HIPAA may surprise you. A bigger misunderstanding, which causes a lot of risks for businesses, is <u>what</u> is covered.

A HIPAA Covered Entity is a medical provider, hospital, or health plan that "conducts certain electronic transactions" related to billing. Electronic transactions include billing health plans, Medicare, and Medicaid for treatment; validating insurance coverage; and paying for treatment.

Many are often surprised to learn that not every doctor has to comply with HIPAA. Those that only accept cash do not have to comply. That doesn't mean that they can release a patient's information without consent, because their license requirements, and sometimes state laws, require confidentiality. However, if they breach patient confidentiality it would not be considered a HIPAA violation.

Health plans are generally thought of as private insurance companies, Medicare, and Medicaid. Some businesses choose to self-fund their health plans by keeping money that would have been spent on insurance premiums, and paying for their employee's healthcare. These businesses are sometimes shocked to find out that they must comply with HIPAA, because they meet the definition of a health plan. We have consulted with school districts, manufacturing companies, and a bank that must comply with HIPAA because of their self-funded health plans.

Protected Health Information (PHI) is anything created, stored, or received by a HIPAA Covered Entity or Business Associate, that is identifiable and contains information about a patient's past, present, or future diagnosis, treatment, or payment. This includes the spoken word, written documents, and electronic data (which is known as ePHI.)

Patients can be identified by things other than their names. HIPAA defines 18 separate identifiers, ranging from specific items like names, medical record numbers, and birthdates, to more general descriptions of age and other characteristics. For example, describing someone as "the driver of NASCAR car 88" would be considered an identifier because it is enough information to identify Dale Earnhardt, Jr.

Besides what is stored in formal medical records, ePHI can include

- E-mail messages and attachments

- Word processing documents

- Spreadsheets

- Reports exported from an EMR system

- Scanned images from copiers and fax systems

- Medical images like X-rays, MRI's, CAT scans, ultrasounds, sonograms

- Photographs

- Voice messages

This data can be stored anywhere - on servers; local computers; the cloud; smartphones and tablets; and removable media like thumb drives, SD cards, and portable hard drives.

State laws protect Social Security and Driver's License numbers. When a receptionist scans an insurance or Medicare card, and a Driver's License, those scanned images must also be secured.

All HIPAA breaches require patient notification, and government reporting. Even a single incident where, for example, a patient receives another patient's bill by mistake. The provider who sent the bill must inform the patient whose bill was seen by the other patient, within 60 days, and must be included in an annual report filed with the government.

Breaches of over 500 records require patient notification, government reporting, and media notices, all within 60 days. These are publicized on a public website nicknamed the 'HIPAA Wall of Shame'.

Since 2009, almost 1,900 incidents have been listed on the Wall of Shame, totaling 173 million patient records.

Here are some popular myths and facts about PHI.

MYTH: We only have to protect our Electronic Medical Records (EMR) system.

MYTH: All our protected data is stored on our servers.

FACT: During our assessments we always surprise our clients by showing them all the locations where their PHI is hiding. We have never found PHI only stored in EMR systems and on servers. Never.

PHI is all over the place, and there are business risks – not just compliance – associated with unmanaged data. We have identified critical data on local computers, laptops, portable media, that was important to the business but wasn't secure, and it wasn't being backed up. It would have been costly to the organization to lose the data.

In many cases the data was on a laptop used by someone who needed to take their data with them, so it wasn't possible to just move the data to a secure server. The laptop needed to be encrypted and added to the backup routine.

We also find PHI on mobile devices, particularly when someone syncs their business email to their phone. Although the free text messaging that comes with a phone isn't either secure or compliant with HIPAA, we have found PHI in text messages. Even by deleting the message from the device does not remove it from the wireless carrier, like ATT & Verizon, nor does it remove it from the other person's phone or wireless carrier.

MYTH: Our EMR system is in the cloud so we don't have to worry about cyber security in our office or on our computers.

FACT: This statement completely fails to consider three important concepts.

1. ALL ePHI, even that outside of the EMR system, must be protected.

2. If you receive e-mail on a local computer, or store files on a local computer, you have PHI outside of your cloud-based EMR system.

3. By far, THE BIGGEST CHALLENGE TO THIS MYTH is that you access your cloud-based EMR system from your local devices.

If your local devices are compromised to steal your password, or piggy-back onto one of your EMR sessions after you log in, the bad guys just gained unauthorized access to your cloud EMR. Many of the biggest hacks have been to compromise someone's password to gain access to medical records.

Even with a cloud EMR system, your local office must be protected by a firewall with active Intrusion Prevention, a domain network, computers with business-class operating systems, current and active anti-virus/anti-malware software, a consistent patching and update process, encryption, and network monitoring.

You either need a skilled IT department or a qualified IT Managed Services company to achieve the level of consistent security and compliance you require.

MYTH – We bought a HIPAA notebook with policies and guidance, so we are compliant.

MYTH – We subscribed to a service with an online portal with training, policies, and a place to store our documents, so we are compliant.

FACTS: Unless you have taken the time to properly learn HIPAA, and fully understand the rules and the enforcement actions, buying 'HIPAA-in-a-Box' may give you a good feeling, but won't adequately protect your organization.

During our assessments, we have had people hand us their policy manuals. When we asked the compliance officers simple questions about the policies, they couldn't answer them. When we asked workforce members about the policies, they were clueless.

In one case, I asked a compliance officer to show me her organization's policies. She took a shrink-wrapped notebook from her shelf, tore off the shrink-wrap, and handed me the book. No one had ever even opened the book, but they had policies!

LESSONS

- **HIPAA is complicated. You need to eat the elephant one bite at a time.**

- **HIPAA covers everything from what staff members do, say, write, access, and share with each other, patients, family members, friends, vendors, the media, and the government.**

- **HIPAA governs the management of ALL paper and electronic data, created, received, or accessed by a HIPAA Covered Entity or Business Associate. This could be as simple as a handwritten note on a napkin, a formal medical record in an Electronic Health Record system, or a voice message.**

- **HIPAA requires about 50 steps to secure technology, but the steps cannot be completed from within an IT department.**

- The HIPAA Breach Reporting Rule requires patient notification and government reporting.

- State laws, industry regulations, contracts, and insurance requirements can alter your compliance program.

- The time to learn HIPAA is not after a breach or compliance violation.

- 'HIPAA-in-a-Box' doesn't work. You must invest time, effort, and money, to properly protect your organization. You can do it yourself, or accelerate your efforts with a consultant.

We have helped hundreds of organizations build compliance programs. Some had already started, and needed some guidance. Others had not done anything, and needed help implementing everything.

We use 'under the skin' tools to analyze networks. We find things others have missed, all the time.

Want to avoid a data breach? Want to validate that your compliance efforts are working? Not sure if your staff really "has HIPAA handled"?

Visit **www.semelconsulting.com** and use the **Contact link.**

Laws, Rules, and other Confusion

The HIPAA & HITECH laws were written by lawmakers for bureaucrats. The HIPAA Privacy, Security, Breach Reporting, and Omnibus rules were written by bureaucrats who had to cover everything from large healthcare systems down to the smallest doctor's office, health plans, and the businesses that work with them. You can read the laws and rules all day and still not understand what they mean.

In 1996 the original HIPAA law was passed by Congress. Its name, the Health Insurance Portability and Accountability Act, reflects its original intent to help workers move to another job without losing their health insurance. The Privacy Rule came out in 2003, and the Security Rule protecting electronic data came into effect in 2005. This was before cloud services, the widespread adoption of electronic medical records, the cloud, and the smart phone.

When the original HIPAA law was written, no one foresaw the number of data breaches that would be caused by Business Associates. No one considered medical record data storage as a cloud service. No one anticipated the costs required to properly enforce compliance. The HITECH Act of 2009 provided funding for enforcement, and included many changes to HIPAA. When the Office for Civil Rights released the 2013 HIPAA Omnibus Final Rule that modified the original HIPAA rules, it required over 500 pages of explanation.

The federal government has tried to help (yes, they really have!) with Frequently Asked Questions and guidance documents. One problem is that some of the outdated questions from 2003 are still on the website.

In the time it took for guidance documents to be released, questions have lingered for years. Many in the healthcare and related industries have had to backtrack to redefine their processes. There are always new issues to interpret, such as what happens when a police officer wearing a body camera walks into an emergency room. This problem is happening now but it is likely to take time for the OCR to gather all the facts it needs, involve legal counsel, coordinate with other agencies, and then issue guidance.

Anyone can report a breach, including patients; employees who either believe in doing the right thing or have an axe to grind with their employer; compliance officers; or senior management. Sometimes breaches are discovered internally. Some are based on patient complaints. Some organizations have learned of breaches when the FBI showed up to tell them their medical records are for sale on the Internet. That's a bad day.

Breaches of over 500 medical records are publicized on a federal website nicknamed "The HIPAA Wall of Shame." Case Resolutions with financial settlements, and Civil Money Penalties with fines (some for breaches of fewer than 500 records) are announced publicly and posted on a federal website. All large breaches are investigated, and most are resolved through a corrective action plan. Some result in large financial settlements, that are well-publicized and used as shining examples of what not to do.

Details of these penalties help you understand the types of incidents that have led to breaches, how the rules are applied, what the enforcers are thinking, and what you may pay if you don't pay attention.

Penalties show us:

- What organizations did to get in trouble

- The underlying causes that set up the circumstances for the breaches

- How the data breaches or compliance violations linked back to the rules

- The value of the penalties, and

- What corrective actions were required to prevent the issue(s) from re-occurring.

Sometimes an enforcement action sends a clear message, but sometimes you have to dig into the wording to find little nuggets to learn. Throughout this book I will take you through penalties and show you what you can do to prevent similar things from hurting you. We will look at the incidents that caused the investigations, and what you can do to avoid a similar expensive and embarrassing experience.

LESSONS

- **Just reading the laws won't teach you HIPAA.**

- **Just reading the rules won't teach you HIPAA.**

- **Just reading the enforcements will give you a better understanding of what you shouldn't do.**

- **You also need to learn what you must do, how the requirements translate into your everyday operations, which could differ greatly from another organization because of your specialty, and even your location.**

- **You need to understand how HIPAA relates to your specific technology, your vendors, your cloud services, and to make sure you aren't secure and compliant just for a moment, but continually.**

You need to work with someone knowledgeable about HIPAA, not just technology or conducting a basic Security Risk Analysis. I have written courses for HIPAA certifications. My blogs have been tweeted out by the Office for Civil Rights. I have spoken at events for the FBI, NASA, and many associations.

Want to avoid a data breach? Want to validate that your compliance efforts are working? Not sure if your staff really "has HIPAA handled"?

Visit www.semelconsulting.com and use the Contact link.

Civil Rights & Real Victims

It's not a coincidence that the HIPAA enforcement agency is called the Office for <u>Civil Rights</u>. Our rights to privacy and confidentiality, and to access our own medical records, are fundamental civil rights.

HIPAA enforcement isn't about taking money from health care providers and health plans, it is about protecting patients' civil rights. Just look at the federal civil rights enforcement in the 1960's to understand what motivates the federal officials who enforce HIPAA.

Data breaches and confidentiality violations are not victimless crimes.

People have been hurt when their medical records were released without authorization, resulting in serious family and relationship problems. I was an expert witness in a lawsuit against a medical facility based on the effects of a confidentiality violation. The impact to the victim was quantified into a seven-figure lawsuit, not just the complaint to the OCR.

Patients whose medical records were stolen and used by criminals to create phony tax returns must deal with long delays in receiving tax refunds. Those whose records were used to create phony credit card accounts, have credit rating nightmares affecting their ability to get credit cards, mortgages, and car loans.

Patients whose HIV and mental health diagnoses were breached have lost their jobs. Some breaches have resulted in extortion, where the patients had to pay to prevent their information from being released to spouses or family members.

Court documents from a lawsuit against Walgreens alleged that Walgreens' customer, whose information was breached, experienced "mental distress, humiliation, and anguish as a result of the breach." The court went on to say that the victim's former boyfriend tried to extort money by "threatening to release the details of her prescription usage to her family unless she abandoned her paternity lawsuit."

In a Connecticut lawsuit, the patient whose data was shared without her authorization testified that the information contained in her breached medical records was used by her ex-boyfriend to file numerous civil actions, including paternity and visitation actions, against her, her attorney, her father and her father's employer, and to threaten her with criminal charges.

LESSONS

- **Remember that every breached record links back to a real person, like you and me.**

- **People have been hurt financially, personally, and emotionally when their info has been breached.**

- **The government has gone to great lengths to protect everyone's Civil Rights.**

INCIDENT – SHASTA REGIONAL MEDICAL CENTER – Shared Patient Information Without Authorization

A patient who had been treated at the Shasta Regional Medical Center (SRMC) went on the record to the California Watch website to question her hospital bill that included treatment for malnutrition. She said no one had discussed that diagnosis, and pointed out that she was, in fact, overweight.

This snowballed into an FBI investigation into the hospital's billing practices, because malnutrition diagnoses at SRMC increased from eight in 2008 to over 1,000 over the next two years.

The hospital's CEO and Chief Medical Officer took the patient's medical records to two newspapers to rebut the story. The CEO also sent an e-mail to the hospital's 785 employees with details of the patient's treatment. The CEO said later that he believed the patient had given up her rights to privacy by discussing her healthcare with the media.

PENALTY – $ 285,000

INCIDENT – New York and Presbyterian Hospital – Authorized TV show to film patients

New York and Presbyterian Hospital (NYP) invited a film crew from the ABC-TV show "NY Med" into its emergency department to film its activities. NYP allowed the crew to film a person who was dying, and another in significant distress, over the objections of at least one medical professional asking the crew to stop.

By inviting the film crew into its treatment areas, it allowed them access to view patients, and overhear conversations, without first getting the patients to authorize disclosure of their medical information.

PENALTY –$ 2.2 million - $ 1.1 million for each patient

LESSONS

- **Medical providers are bound by rules that do not apply to their patients.**

Patients can do whatever they want with their medical information. They can share it with friends, discuss it on social media sites, and with the media.

The patient's actions do not change the rules that if a Covered Entity wants to share their information, other than for treatment, payment, business operations, or for other limited reasons, they must first obtain written authorization from the patient.

- **The media may not enter patient areas for filming. Patient rights are protected automatically; you can't ask for permission later. You have no way to know who might file a complaint.**

It is not permissible for a film crew to record a patient and then try to mask their identity, blur their faces, etc. The patients had a civil right not to be filmed in the first place unless they had already signed an authorization. The OCR has issued a guidance document making this very clear.

In the OCR's press release about the settlement, it says that filming continued "even after a medical professional urged the crew to stop." Did the medical professional turn in the hospital for the HIPAA violation? Was the professional a hospital employee, or perhaps an ambulance attendant who dropped off a patient and witnessed the situation? Or was it a distraught family member?

It could have been any of them, since anyone can report a breach. Remember, patient rights are civil rights.

You need guidance from someone knowledgeable about HIPAA, not just about conducting a basic Security Risk Analysis. I have written courses for HIPAA certifications. My blogs have been tweeted out by the Office for Civil Rights. I have spoken at events for the FBI, NASA, and many associations.

Want to avoid a data breach? Want to validate that your compliance efforts are working? Not sure if your staff really "has HIPAA handled"?

Visit www.semelconsulting.com and use the Contact link.

Free and Easy can be Very Expensive & Difficult

We love free. Free e-mail accounts. Free texting. Free cloud storage.

We love easy. Easy to communicate. Easy to access. Easy to share.

Health care providers are no different than anyone else. Free and Easy are good, right?

NO. Free and easy can be very expensive and difficult.

Consumer-grade free e-mail, texting, and cloud services do not include the required security and compliance required for HIPAA. Vendors will not sign Business Associate Agreements (BAA) for their free services. BAA's are a requirement made crystal clear in the October, 2016, OCR guidance that any cloud service storing data is a HIPAA Business Associate.

Google is a great company. Its search engine is phenomenal. I have a free Gmail account I use for personal correspondence. I use Google Photos to share family pictures. But I never put anything in Google I wouldn't want the world to see, because to get the free services **Google required me to agree that it can read, and even publish, anything I store in their services.**

> **Google Terms & Conditions** https://www.google.com/intl/ en/policies/terms/
>
> **Your Content in our Services**

Some of our Services allow you to upload, submit, store, send or receive content. You retain ownership of any intellectual property rights that you hold in that content. In short, what belongs to you stays yours.

When you upload, submit, store, send or receive content to or through our Services, you give Google (and those we work with) a worldwide license to use, host, store, **reproduce**, modify, create derivative works (such as those resulting from translations, adaptations or other changes we make so that your content works better with our Services), **communicate, publish...**

Vendors like Google, DropBox, Box.com, and others that offer free data storage, usually have a paid version of their services that are secure and for which they will sign a BAA.

Remember, if it's free, it could end up being VERY expensive.

INCIDENT – PHOENIX CARDIAC SURGERY – used unapproved and non-compliant free cloud e-mail and calendar service

Over a four-year period, the medical practice used free Internet-based cloud e-mail services to communicate PHI. For two years, the practice used a publicly accessible free on-line calendar to schedule over 1,000 patient visits. No Business Associate Agreements were signed with the online services.

During its investigation, the OCR discovered that the medical practice:

- Failed to provide HIPAA training to its workforce

- Failed to implement safeguards to protect PHI

- Failed to appoint a security official

- Failed to conduct a Security Risk Analysis

- Failed to manage its Business Associate relationships

PENALTY – $ 100,000

INCIDENT - OREGON HEALTH & SCIENCE UNIVERSITY - lost laptop & sharing ePHI on a free Internet service

Oregon Health & Science University (OHSU) reported a stolen laptop. Three months later, while OCR was investigating the laptop incident, OHSU reported that its workforce members were using a third-party Internet service for storing ePHI.

During its investigation OCR discovered that OHSU

- Failed to encrypt ePHI

- Failed to implement policies and procedures to protect PHI

- Failed to manage its Business Associate Relationships

PENALTY - $ 2.7 million

LESSONS

- **Only use cloud services that are secure and will sign a HIPAA Business Associate Agreement.**

- **Make sure that your cloud service accounts are corporate accounts, and not set up individually by your workforce members.**

- **Implement and update security policies and train your workforce. Learn from previous penalties.**

In October, 2016, the OCR released a guidance document validating that cloud services and data centers are HIPAA Business Associates, even if they never access PHI, even if it is encrypted, and stored in locked cages. Until then, many cloud services and data centers denied that they were Business Associates, and refused to sign Business Associate Agreements.

When HIPAA came out in 2003, there was no such thing as the cloud. So, organizations never included the possibility of using a cloud service in their security policies. One of the requirements of the HIPAA Security Rule is called Evaluation. It requires that an organization's security policies be reviewed periodically to ensure that they meet the current needs of the organization. Through Evaluation you can identify that your existing policies don't cover new challenges like cloud services, giving you the opportunity to update your policies and train your workforce to comply, rather than unknowingly creating an expensive risk and compliance violation.

During one of our security risk analyses we discovered software on computers for a popular cloud sharing service. The client was unaware that staff members were using the free service, and contacted the service to set up a corporate account for the paid version that is secure and for which the company will sign a Business Associate Agreement.

We had identified six computers and knew the user's names. When our client called the cloud service to ask them to switch the accounts to the corporate account, they received some disturbing information.

The cloud service said that, even though the workforce members had set up their account using their work e-mail addresses, the cloud service considered the data to be their personal property. The cloud service told our client that their workforce members would have to request the transfer of their data to the corporate account. Our client was shocked that his workforce members took ownership of the organization's data, without authorization and without the organization even being aware.

Worse, we had identified six workforce members, but the cloud service said there were other accounts with data in their system, also set up with the organization's e-mail accounts. These were created by employees no longer associated with the organization, and who did not respond when they were contacted. Whatever data they stored was lost to the organization forever.

After seeing that OHSU paid $ 2.7 million, and a small medical practice paid $ 100,000, aren't you wondering how well your staff knows not to use free Internet e-mail and storage services?

We use 'under the skin' tools to analyze networks. We often find users sharing files on free services.

Want to avoid a data breach? Want to validate that your compliance efforts are working? Not sure if your staff really "has HIPAA handled"?

Visit www.semelconsulting.com and use the Contact link.

Business Associates: Trusted Vendors, or Huge Business Risks?

Business Associate relationships can be complicated. New guidance makes it clear that a vendor that does not even look at medical records is a Business Associate. Subcontractors of Business Associates are also Business Associates. This means a Covered Entity needs to make sure that its Business Associates are signing Business Associate Agreements with <u>their</u> subcontractors, who are signing Business Associate Agreements with <u>their</u> subcontractors.

Confusing? Here is a real-life example.

A doctor's office (HIPAA Covered Entity) buys online backup services from a local IT company. The IT company resells a cloud service. The cloud service has its computers in a secure data center.

- The doctor signs a Business Associate Agreement with the IT company

- The IT company signs a Subcontractor Business Associate Agreement with the cloud service

- The cloud service signs a Subcontractor Business Associate Agreement with the data center

How far does you go? Keep going down the line until you see where the data stops.

Since HIPAA was introduced in 2003, a key component has been the ability for Covered Entities to share PHI with Business Associates - vendors, partners, parent companies, and other non-Covered Entities whose services require access to medical records. In some circumstances a Covered Entity can have a relationship with another Covered Entity that makes it a Business Associate.

All that was required was a signed Business Associate Agreement limiting what the Business Associate could do with the PHI, and requiring that it be secured and kept confidential.

At the time HIPAA was written, no one envisioned how many data breaches would be caused by Business Associates. The original HIPAA law did not give the government the ability to fine Business Associates. In 2009, the HITECH Act gave the government that power, and required Business Associates to implement full compliance programs. This did not take effect until the 2013 HIPAA Omnibus Final Rule was released.

The new rule included requirements for subcontractors of Business Associates, and clarified that organizations that store data are Business Associates, even if they do not look at the data. This requirement included cloud service providers, online backup companies, and data centers.

The Minnesota Attorney General and the Federal Trade Commission didn't wait until 2013 to go after Accretive, which cost the company over $ 600 million, and cost the CEO and CFO their jobs.

Since 2009, over 28 million patient records have been breached by Business Associates.

In 2016, for the first time, a Business Associate paid a HIPAA penalty to the government.

Although compliance is required by law, it is surprising at the casual approach we often see with Business Associate relationships. Medical practices do not require their vendors to sign Business Associate Agreements and comply with the law. Business Associates have told their customers that they are "HIPAA-compliant" even though they have not implemented required compliance programs, or provided required HIPAA training to their employees.

INCIDENT – Care New England Health System (CNE) – lost backup tapes, shared PHI with a member hospital without an updated Business Associate Agreement

Woman & Infant's Hospital of Rhode Island (WIH), a member of the Care New England Health System, reported that unencrypted backup tapes containing ePHI were missing from two of its facilities. CNE provides IT services to the hospitals under its ownership and control, but is a separate company from the hospital and is in fact a Business Associate of the hospitals it owns.

During its investigation, the OCR determined that CNE had not updated its Business Associate Agreement with its member hospitals, as required by the 2013 HIPAA Omnibus Final Rule. By not having a current agreement in place, sharing information between the hospitals and their parent company met the definition of a data breach.

PENALTY - $ 400,000

INCIDENT – Catholic Health Care Services – lost iPhone with 412 nursing home resident records

Catholic Health Care Services (CHCS), part of the Philadelphia diocese, provided management and IT services to six skilled nursing facilities. One of its employees lost an unencrypted iPhone containing 412 resident records, including Social Security numbers, information regarding diagnosis and treatment, medical procedures, names of family members and legal guardians, and medication information.

The OCR's investigation revealed that CHCS had not conducted a Security Risk Analysis, and had not implemented security policies and procedures to protect ePHI.

PENALTY - $ 650,000

INCIDENT – Cottage Health System – IT vendor published patient records to the Internet

Cottage Health System hired an IT Managed Services Provider to install a server, which it accidently published to the Internet, exposing over 32,000 patient records to Google searches.

Cottage Health used its insurance coverage to receive legal representation and settle a $ 4.1 million class action suit with its patients. Court documents from a lawsuit filed by Columbia Casualty, Cottage Health System's insurer, said the IT Managed Service Provider did "not maintain sufficient liquid assets to contribute towards the proposed settlement fund and does not maintain liability insurance that applies with respect to the privacy claims asserted in the Underlying Action."

Resolution: The lawsuit was thrown out by a judge because Columbia Casualty had not first attempted arbitration to settle the dispute, as required in its policy.

INCIDENT – Accretive Health – lost laptop

In September, 2011, North Memorial Health Care reported that an unencrypted laptop belonging to Accretive Health, its Business Associate, was stolen from an Accretive employee's car. 23,000 patient records were lost.

This triggered an investigation that resulted in a $ 1.55 million penalty against the hospital, because the investigation revealed it shared 289,904 records with Accretive without having first signed a Business Associate Agreement.

Business Associates were not yet directly liable for data breaches through the HIPAA regulations, so the Minnesota State Attorney General and the Federal Trade Commission went after Accretive.

A broad investigation by the Attorney General found that Accretive had deceived patients, harassed them for money in emergency rooms, and mishandled data (citing the lost laptop). Accretive paid a fine and was banned from doing business in Minnesota for 2 – 6 years.

At the same time, the Federal Trade Commission in its quest to protect consumers against "fraudulent, deceptive, and unfair business practices," placed Accretive on a 20-year monitored compliance program.

The CEO and CFO were replaced, shareholders filed a class-action suit, and Accretive Health's stock was de-listed from the New York Stock Exchange.

PENALTY – $ 1.55 million against North Memorial Health Care

$ 2.5 million state fine, and agreement not to do business in Minnesota for 2-6 years

Financial Impact – ACCRETIVE LOST $ 668 MILLION IN VALUE

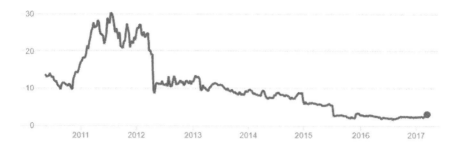

This chart shows the drop from June, 2011, when Accretive Health stock sold for $ 30 per share, to 2017, when its stock is worth $ 2.50 per share. The high point was just before the lost laptop was reported.

LESSONS –

- **It may not make sense at first, but a management company that owns medical practices, hospitals, skilled nursing facilities, and other HIPAA Covered Entities, is a Business Associate of the organizations it owns. A management company must implement a full HIPAA compliance program, that addresses the services it provides, and how it comes in contact with PHI.**

  If you work for a management company, you may think of yourself as part of the Covered Entity you support. You may work all day seemingly as part of the medical practice, hospital, or skilled nursing facility. However, the division between corporations means the Covered Entity is sharing PHI with you, an employee of another company.

  This also applies to facilities that outsource departments. When I was the CIO at a hospital with a skilled nursing facility, we outsourced our food service. The food service manager, dieticians, and kitchen help were all employed by the food service. They had full access to our patient records so they could prepare food according to the patients' dietary restrictions. The food service manager attended all of our department head meetings, and everyone in the department acted as though they were hospital employees. We had a Business Associate Agreement in place with the food service vendor.

  We have worked with many types of HIPAA Business Associates. Some have minimal contact with PHI, while others store millions of patient records. Some of the Business Associates with whom we have worked are healthcare-focused businesses, while others have no healthcare training or experience.

  It has been a challenge with some Business Associates to build compliance programs, which has been compounded by state law requirements, contracts and data use agreements, and insurance requirements.

- **Choose qualified vendors.**

- **Make HIPAA compliance a deal-breaker in your vendor-selection process**

- **Demand proof of compliance, or an independent audit**

- **Validate that your Business Associates carry Professional Liability (also known as Errors & Omission) Insurance, that meets a minimum amount you require, and that you get an insurance certificate naming your organization as a named insured on their policy.**

- Choosing qualified vendors is difficult if you are not familiar with their industry. However, it doesn't take much web surfing to see what other businesses are doing, and what industry and vendor certifications are available.

Was the IT company selected by Cottage Health to install its server certified by the manufacturer? Did its technicians and engineers have vendor and industry certifications?

My business card and e-mail signature both list certifications I have earned. Our company worked hard to earn CompTIA's Security Trustmark Plus, and its logo is on our business cards, proposals, and website. We have distinguished ourselves against others who talk about HIPAA and cyber security, but have not earned the certifications proving it.

Would you rather be treated by a board-certified doctor with years of experience, who has performed hundreds of procedures, or someone who just talks about what they have done?

In today's world where billboards and TV ads solicit you to sue for car accidents, medical malpractice, medication complications, asbestos exposure, and so many other reasons, I find it inconceivable that an IT company would not carry a reasonable amount of Errors & Omission insurance.

I have owned IT companies and our insurance coverage was governed by what our clients required, not what I thought might be an adequate amount to satisfy my tolerance for risk. We once had a client that demanded we have $ 7 million in coverage. Our insurance company would not sell me that amount of coverage, so we put them in touch with our client, who agreed to a lower amount. Every time I renewed our insurance I made sure our carrier provided our clients with the insurance certificates listing them as a named insured.

It doesn't matter if your organization is small. You need to be protected by your vendors against regulatory penalties, and litigation they might cause. Demand proof of insurance before you sign an agreement, and make sure proof of ongoing coverage, and notification if they cancel coverage, is a requirement in your contracts.

We have helped many types of Business Associates build compliance programs and protect themselves. We have also helped healthcare clients identify vendors who talked about HIPAA but were not compliant.

Want to avoid a data breach? Want to validate that your compliance efforts are working? Not sure if your staff really "has HIPAA handled"?

Visit www.semelconsulting.com and use the Contact link.

Don't be a Slow Learner... a Clock is Ticking (somewhere)

The HIPAA Security Rule is all about implementing effective risk management to adequately and effectively protect EPHI.

National Institute of Standards & Technology (NIST)

To comply with HIPAA, you must continue to review, correct or modify, and update security protections.

Office of the National Coordinator for Health Information Technology

You can't ignore or keep delaying risk management. Organizations have paid millions in fines while trying to save thousands in remediation.

There are always clocks ticking in the background with HIPAA. Some are specific, like the 60-day limit on notifying patients after a data breach. Others are vague, with case resolutions against organizations that knew they had to conduct a security risk analysis, or remediate known security issues, but didn't correct them within a 'reasonable' timeframe.

We could argue what is 'reasonable' for a long time, but it doesn't matter what we think. Here are some examples that show what the HIPAA enforcers think.

INCIDENT – Concentra Health Care – lost laptop, failure to remediate known problems

Concentra, a company that owns urgent care and physical therapy centers, had an unencrypted laptop stolen from a Missouri physical therapy center, breaching 870 patient records.

The investigation revealed that Concentra had conducted a Security Risk Analysis and identified the risk to data on unencrypted laptops. However, from October, 2008, until the breach occurred in late 2011, Concentra had only encrypted 434 of its 597 laptops.

The resolution agreement stated that Concentra had "failed to adequately execute risk management measures to reduce its identified lack of encryption."

PENALTY –$ 1.725 million

INCIDENT - Oregon Health & Science University (OHSU) - multiple violations, failure to remediate known problems

First, OHSU reported a stolen laptop. Then, four months later, while the laptop theft was being investigated by the OCR, OHSU notified the OCR that members of its workforce were storing ePHI on an Internet-based service without a Business Associate Agreement.

In its press release, the OCR said, "OHSU performed risk analyses in 2003, 2005, 2006, 2008, 2010, and 2013, but OCR's investigation found that these analyses did not cover all ePHI in OHSU's enterprise, as required by the Security Rule. While the analyses identified vulnerabilities and risks to ePHI located in many areas of the organization, OHSU did not act in a timely manner to implement measures to address these documented risks and vulnerabilities to a reasonable and appropriate level."

PENALTY - $ 2.7 million

INCIDENT – Presence Health Network – failure to notify patients within the required timeframe

On January 31, 2014, a Presence Health affiliated hospital notified the OCR that on October 22, 2013, it had lost paper-based operating room schedules containing PHI for 836 patients. Presence told the OCR that miscommunications caused a delay in reporting the breach. Based on the 60-day HIPAA reporting requirement, Presence should have reported breach by December 21, 2013. They were 41 days late reporting to the federal government.

Presence did not notify their patients until February 3, 2014, 104 days after discovering the breach. They notified the media 106 days after discovering the breach.

During the OCR investigation, which often take years to complete, Presence Health reported additional breaches of fewer than 500 patient records. While investigating those smaller breaches, the OCR discovered that Presence was not compliant with the requirement to provide timely written notifications to the affected patients.

From its press release: "Covered entities need to have a clear policy and procedures in place to respond to the Breach Notification Rule's timeliness requirements" said OCR Director Jocelyn Samuels. "Individuals need prompt notice of a breach of their unsecured PHI so they can take action that could help mitigate any potential harm caused by the breach."

PENALTY - $ 475,000

INCIDENT – MAPFRE Life Insurance Company – failure to implement corrective measures it informed the OCR it would undertake

In September, 2011, MAPFRE Life Insurance Company of Puerto Rico, reported that an unencrypted 'pen drive' containing 2,209 records was stolen from its IT department.

During its investigation, the OCR discovered that MAPFRE failed to conduct an accurate and thorough Security Risk Analysis, failed to manage its risks, failed to implement a security awareness and training program for its staff, failed to encrypt ePHI, and failed to implement appropriate HIPAA policies.

In other words, MAPFRE did not do much, if anything, to comply with HIPAA.

In its press release, the OCR accuses MAPFRE of "a **failure to conduct its risk analysis and implement risk management plans,** *contrary to its prior representations*, and **a failure to deploy encryption** or an equivalent alternative measure on its laptops and removable storage media **until September 1, 2014. MAPFRE also failed to implement or delayed implementing other corrective measures it informed OCR it would undertake.**"

This indicates that the OCR had accepted MAPFRE's commitment to conduct a risk analysis, manage its risks, and to encrypt its devices, as part of a Corrective Action Plan to avoid a financial penalty.

By failing to follow through on its commitments to the OCR, MAPFRE paid over $ 2 million.

"Covered entities must not only make assessments to safeguard ePHI, they must act on those assessments as well" said OCR Director Jocelyn Samuels.

PENALTY - $ 2.2 million

INCIDENT – Children's Medical Center – failure to remedy known issues

Children's Medical Center, of Dallas, (CMC) knew it needed to encrypt data as far back as 2007, based on a Security Gap Analysis. It submitted that report to the OCR in 2010 during a breach investigation. In 2008, another risk analysis had identified unencrypted devices as a critical vulnerability.

Even knowing the risks, starting in 2007, CMC began issuing unencrypted BlackBerry devices to its nursing staff, and continued to allow workers to use unencrypted laptops to store PHI.

In August, 2011, CMC reported that in December, 2010, eight months earlier, a medical resident lost an iPod that contained 22 patient records.

In July, 2013, CMC reported the theft of an unencrypted laptop containing 2,462 medical records, from a storage area accessible by staff members, some of whom were not authorized to access PHI.

PENALTY – $ 3.2 million

Almost all HIPAA penalties are negotiated case resolutions, where the Covered Entity or Business Associate cooperates with the investigators, and participates in a settlement discussion.

This enforcement was a Civil Money Penalty of **$ 1.695 million, calculated at $ 1,000 per day** against CMC for failure to address encryption when it should have. In addition, CMC was fined **$ 1,000 per patient for each medical record** it lost.

Unlike most HIPAA penalties that are negotiated case resolutions, where the Covered Entity or Business Associate cooperates with the investigators, and participates in a settlement discussion, this enforcement was a Civil Money Penalty of **$ 1.695 million, calculated at $ 1,000 per day** against CMC for failure to address encryption when it should have. In addition, CMC was fined **$ 1,000 per patient for each medical record** it lost.

LESSONS

- **When you identify a risk, you must address it.**

    Identify and locate all the data you own, and assess the threats and vulnerabilities that can affect its security.

- **Conduct annual risk assessments, and update them when anything significant changes.**

- **When you become aware of a problem, fix it. Don't ignore risks, and just keep identifying them in reports year after year.**

- **Have an Incident Management and Breach Reporting plan in place, ready to grab as soon as something happens. Once an incident occurs you should not be trying to formulate a plan. Delays should not occur because of miscommunications.**

- **Understand and communicate the rules.**

- **Make sure everyone knows the patient and government reporting requirements. Some states have laws that require patient notification in less than the 60 days permitted by HIPAA.**

- **Time is never on your side.**

- **Identify and locate all the data you own, and assess the threats and vulnerabilities that can affect its security.**

Identifying what data you have, and where it is located, is more difficult than it seems. We are often told that "all of our protected data is on our server" or "all of our protected data is in our EHR system." We use tools to search for data, and over the years we have developed a sense that has helped us locate data in some unusual places. Clients have been shocked to have us show them where their data is hiding, and we have determined that some business-critical data has not been properly tracked and is not being backed up. If the device failed, or was lost or stolen, the unrecoverable data would be lost forever.

When you work in an enterprise, which could be spread across just a few Offices; or a large health system with multiple campuses, clinics, medical offices, across a wide geography; it is difficult to conduct a comprehensive security risk analysis. It takes assessment skills, assessment experience, assessment tools, and time, – resources that many IT departments don't have.

Security and compliance are not about reports; they are about addressing your risks and protecting the confidentiality of your patients and customers.

When a vulnerability is identified, it must be addressed quickly. How can you possibly know the moment an attack may occur against that vulnerability? How do you know you aren't under attack right now?

It doesn't make a lot of sense to pay for risk reports that identify security gaps, not fix them, and then provide those reports to a government agency that is investigating you. Security risk analyses will always find something that needs fixing. Fix your problems, and document your activities, so if you do suffer a breach, you can show the investigators that you had good intentions and took your responsibilities seriously.

It is critical that management provide adequate resources, including money, staff, and time, to support security and compliance.

I can understand a Chief Financial Officer or financial controller not wanting to have all the encryption expenses hit in the same fiscal quarter. (At the time Concentra lost the laptop, it was owned by Humana, a public company.) But waiting 3 years? When you consider the cost to install encryption, including labor, was probably $ 150 per laptop, Concentra could have avoided the $ 1.725 million penalty by spending under $ 25,000.

Maybe it was an overworked Chief Information Officer or IT Director who decided to pace out the encryption project and fit it in whenever his staff had time. Having been in that position, I understand the temptation. However, when it came to security and compliance risks, I had to bring in outside vendors to get projects done in a short timeframe. Our department wasn't staffed to handle big projects, and take care of our hospital's everyday needs.

I bet OHSU management wishes it had invested in a HIPAA-compliant file sharing solution, and trained its staff to use it. It would have cost a fraction of the $ 2.7 million penalty.

I bet CMC management wishes it had invested a fraction of its $ 3.2 million fine in encrypting its devices, so it could have used the money for helping children.

I bet MAPFRE's management wishes it had paid attention to what it was telling the OCR it would do, to avoid a financial penalty, rather than paying over $ 2 million for failing to keep its word.

We have helped many types of Business Associates build compliance programs and protect themselves. We have also helped healthcare clients identify vendors who talked about HIPAA but were not compliant.

Want to avoid a data breach? Want to validate that your compliance efforts are working? Not sure if your staff really "has HIPAA handled"?

Visit www.semelconsulting.com and use the Contact link.

Data is Worth More than Gold

If you think of DATA as GOLD, and stop thinking of data as bits and bytes, you will do a better job protecting your organization.

Gold has a high value. So do medical records.

Gold needs to be secured. So do medical records.

Gold is something criminals want to steal. Like medical records.

Gold is worth over $ 1,200 per ounce. Medical records are worth much more.

INCIDENT - Adult & Pediatric Dermatology - lost thumb drive

Adult & Pediatric Dermatology (APD), a Massachusetts-based dermatology and plastic surgery clinic, reported the theft of a thumb drive from the vehicle of one of its workforce members. Approximately 2,200 patient records were lost. It reported the breach and notified its patients.

During its investigation, the OCR discovered that APD had failed to conduct an accurate and thorough security risk analysis, failed to implement written policies and procedures, failed to train its workforce, and failed to encrypt devices containing PHI.

PENALTY - $ 150,000

INCIDENT – Catholic Health Care Services – lost iPhone

Catholic Health Care Services (CHCS), part of the Philadelphia diocese, provided management and IT services to six skilled nursing facilities. One of its employees lost an unencrypted iPhone containing 412 resident records, including Social Security numbers, information regarding diagnosis and treatment, medical procedures, names of family members and legal guardians, and medication information.

The OCR's investigation revealed that CHCS had not conducted a Security Risk Analysis, and had not implemented security policies and procedures to protect ePHI.

PENALTY - $ 650,000

INCIDENT - MAPFRE Life Insurance Company - stolen 'pen drive'

In September, 2011, MAPFRE Life Insurance Company of Puerto Rico, reported that an unencrypted 'pen drive' containing 2,209 records was stolen from its IT department.

During its investigation, the OCR discovered that MAPFRE failed to conduct an accurate and thorough Security Risk Analysis, failed to manage its risks, failed to implement a security awareness and training program for its staff, failed to encrypt ePHI, and failed to implement appropriate HIPAA policies.

PENALTY - $ 2.2 million

LESSONS

- **Data is worth more than gold.**

- **Think of data as gold**

- **If you think of someone whose job it is to protect gold, you may do a better job protecting data**

The price of gold on the world market is just over $ 1,250 per ounce.

A thumb drive weighs ¾ of one ounce.

An iPhone weights 4.9 ounces.

If the Adult & Pediatric Dermatology thumb drive was made of solid gold, it would be worth $ 937.

They paid a $ 150,000 penalty.

If the Catholic Health Care Service's iPhone was solid gold, it would be worth $ 6,125.

They paid a $ 650,000 penalty.

If the MAPFRE pen drive was solid gold, it would be worth $ 937.

They paid a $ 2.2 million penalty.

Visualizing your data as gold is a great way to communicate that it has value. There are people who want to steal it, it has value to your organization for business reasons, and you could pay a high penalty if it is lost.

If you can convince your decision-makers that data is worth more than gold, they may provide you with the resources you need for security and compliance.

Want to send the message to your staff with a FREE COLOR SIGN showing a laptop with gold bars on the screen?

Want to avoid a data breach? Want to validate that your compliance efforts are working? Not sure if your staff really "has HIPAA handled"?

Visit www.semelconsulting.com and use the Contact link.

I Googled Myself and Found My Medical Records

That's a bad day, and it happens a lot more than it should.

File and data base servers can be set up for secure access by authorized users, or as Internet platforms for use by the public. Google and other search engines constantly scan the Internet for information. Whether Google adds the latest news article, or a patient's medical records, to its search engine, is simply based on how the servers were set up.

INCIDENT – Wellpoint – shared health plan member info on web portal

In 2010, Wellpoint, a parent company of multiple health plans, was made aware of a HIPAA data breach when it was sued by an applicant who discovered she could access the records of other health plan members.

In a press release announcing the class action settlement, the Orange County Superior Court said,

> "The lawsuit alleges that from approximately October 23, 2009, to March 10, 2010, WellPoint/Anthem Blue Cross improperly stored personal information and electronic versions of individual health insurance applications for over 600,000 customers, enrollees or subscribers on its web-based servers without username, password and encryption protections.
>
> This information included personal identifying information and personal health information, such as Social Security numbers, home and office addresses, telephone numbers, credit card numbers and financial information used for premium payments, and other information people may have provided on their health insurance applications. The lawsuit alleges that WellPoint/Anthem Blue Cross did not adequately protect this information. WellPoint/Anthem Blue Cross denies the claims in the lawsuit. The class settlement does not mean that WellPoint/Anthem Blue Cross did anything wrong."

The OCR investigation revealed that WellPoint did not properly secure access to its databases, due to a software upgrade that affected its security. WellPoint did not properly evaluate the software upgrade to determine what it could to, failed to implement technology to limit access only to authorized people, disclosing the Social Security Numbers and health information of 612,000 people.

PENALTY – $ 1.7 million

INCIDENT – Skagit County, Washington – accidently published patient info to the Internet

The Skagit County government reported that it had accidently published seven receipts for medical tests on a publicly-accessible server.

The OCR investigation discovered that the PHI of 1,581 individuals – not seven- was available through the Internet. The county had not notified all the patients affected within the timeframe required by the Breach Notification Rule.

From the time the HIPAA Security Rule came into effect in 2005, until 2014, the county government had not implemented HIPAA policies, data security, and had not trained its employees.

The county had done little or nothing to comply with HIPAA, even though its Public Health department provides services for:

> Mental Health Care
> Substance Abuse Treatment
> Maternity & Child Health Care
> Communicable Diseases
> Developmental Disabilities
> Senior Nutrition

PENALTY - $ 215,000 (taxpayer funds, almost $ 2 per resident based on the county population of 118,000)

INCIDENT - NY & Presbyterian & Columbia University Medical Center - accidently published patient information to the Internet

This breach makes me shake my head in wonder.

Would two leading hospitals allow an IT tech to treat a patient? Of course not.

So, why would two leading hospitals allow a *doctor* to install *a personally-owned server* on its network, and accidently share the PHI of 6,800 people to the Internet?

New York & Presbyterian (NYP), and Columbia University Medical Center (CU), are two separate HIPAA Covered Entities that have an arrangement for CU faculty members to serve as attending physicians at NYP. They share a data network and network firewall, which link to PHI for NYP patients.

The hospitals learned of the breach after receiving a complaint that a former patient's PHI was available on the Internet. The information included patient status, vital signs, medications, and lab results.

The investigation revealed that a physician, who had developed software applications for the hospital, had attempted to deactivate his personally-owned server, resulting in PHI being accessible on Internet search engines. Neither hospital had checked the server to make sure it was secure and properly protected.

Nor had the hospitals conducted an accurate and thorough risk analysis that identified all the systems that accessed PHI, like the doctor's personally-owned server.

The investigation also determined that NYP had failed to comply with its own policies on access management.

PENALTIES –New York & Presbyterian Hospital - $ 3.3 million

Columbia University Medical Center - $ 1.5 million

INCIDENT - Complete PT - published patient testimonials and photos on website without authorization

Complete PT, a physical therapy clinic, posted patient testimonials, including full names and full face photographs, on its website, without obtaining HIPAA-compliant authorizations.

The OCR investigation revealed that Complete PT had failed to implement appropriate HIPAA policies related to the release of patient information, and to safeguard PHI.

PENALTY - $ 25,000

LESSONS

- **It is easy to accidently configure a file server to make its data accessible to the Internet.**

- **It takes a certified network engineer to properly deploy and retire a file server to protect against the loss or unauthorized access of PHI**

- **Portals are great ways to make information available to clients, patients, health plan members**

- **To ensure that a secure server is not published to the Internet, it requires:**
  - **The person setting up the server should be certified by the software vendor**
  - **They should identify what steps are required to publish the server to the Internet**
  - **They should create a checklist making sure NONE of the steps to publish the server to the Internet are taken**
  - **At the go-live moment they should check to be sure the server is not accessible through the Internet**

We have helped many types of Covered Entities and Business Associates build compliance programs and protect themselves by following our checklists for system deployments and retirements, and to check their systems to ensure that PHI is not accessible through the Internet.

Want to avoid a data breach? Want to validate that your compliance efforts are working? Not sure if your staff really "has HIPAA handled"?

Visit www.semelconsulting.com and use the Contact link.

You Lost WHAT??? It was encrypted, RIGHT???

Data is everywhere.

It is simply amazing how many multi-million dollar fines are paid because of lost UNENCRYPTED devices.

Encryption seals data from being accessed without authorization, and a lost ENCRYPTED device is EXEMPT from breach reporting rules. A LOST ENCRYPTED DEVICE DOES NOT HAVE TO BE REPORTED AS A BREACH.

New computers, tablets, and smartphones include encryption for free. It is not expensive to encrypt an older device. So why do so many organizations pay more than $ 1 million in fines when they could have spent $ 100 on encryption?

By far, the greatest number of incidents reported (49%) were for lost or stolen unencrypted devices. While 75% of breached medical records have been caused by hackers, hacking only accounts for 15% of the number of breaches reported. The California Attorney General reported that lost or stolen devices accounted for over 70% of the breaches reported to the state.

There are so many different types of devices that can store data, from network servers with hundreds of hard drives down to micro SD cards the size of your fingernail. While you may think data is always stored on computers, many people have business e-mails with attachments sent to their smartphones, and telephone systems now store messages and forward them as e-mail attachments.

HIPAA's Breach Reporting Rule requires that all lost or stolen unencrypted devices be reported. The Wall of Shame categorizes the types of devices that have been reported, although many fall into a category called Other Portable Electronic Devices.

It's not surprising to see the long list of laptops that have been lost or stolen. What is surprising is to see that almost 200 incidents were caused by lost or stolen <u>network servers</u> and <u>desktop</u> computers.

There are many ways to prevent devices from being lost or stolen, and from data being breached the loss or theft occurs.

The simplest and one of the least expensive ways to protect data is with device encryption. Encryption seals protected data so that it cannot be accessed without an encryption key. The HIPAA Breach Reporting Rule, and almost all state laws, exempt encrypted data that has been lost or stolen from being reported as a breach.

If a password-protected unencrypted hard drive is removed from a computer and attached as a second drive to another computer, you can get to its data without knowing the password. Encrypted drives seal the protected data in a 'container' that cannot be accessed without an encryption key. Removing the drive and connecting it as a second drive on another system will not allow access to the data.

Older computers did not come with encryption, which had to be purchased separately. Today's Windows and Macintosh operating systems include encryption, which can simply be turned on.

If you have older computers, you should buy encryption, which usually costs around $ 100 per computer. On newer computers, you need to make sure your IT department or IT vendor has turned on encryption and verified it is working. This is likely the least expensive insurance against data breaches that you can buy.

One thing to remember is that the time you decide not to report a missing computer because it is encrypted, is after it is gone. How can you prove it was encrypted when it was stolen? Business-class encryption and network management tools can check the devices in your organization and create reports showing encryption is installed and active. You should archive these reports so you can produce one as evidence if you lose an encrypted device and decide not to report it.

Because this is the most common way to breach data, it should be at the top of your list to address.

INCIDENT – Advocate Health System – stolen computers, Business Associate hacked, laptop stolen from employee's car

2013 was a bad year for Advocate Health System's patients. In July, four unencrypted laptops were stolen from a suburban Chicago office. Later in the summer, one of its Business Associates was accessed by an unauthorized user. Finally, in November, Advocate reported yet another theft of a laptop computer, from an employee's car. What was remarkable about these breaches was that 4 million patient records were breached.

Advocate's system is the major health care provider in the Chicago region, with 12 hospitals, 1,000 doctors, and 200 locations.

The obvious question is why 4 million records were stored on 4 unencrypted laptops in a suburban office of a large health system – an office that did not have an alarm system.

At first, Advocate claimed that only names, addresses, Social Security Numbers, and birthdates were lost. Weeks later it corrected its claim to admit that medical diagnoses, medical record number, medical treatment codes, and health insurance information was included.

What may have been the Understatement of the Year was when an Advocate executive said that the data should not have been stored on the computers.

"This type of data should always be maintained on our secure network," said Kelly Jo Golson, Sr. Vice President of Advocate.

You think???

PENALTY - $ 5.5 million

INCIDENT – Blue Cross Blue Shield of Tennessee – stolen servers and hard drives

In 2009, an employee of Blue Cross/Blue Shield of Tennessee (BCBST) discovered the theft of computer equipment, including servers and 57 hard drives containing 300,000 videos and over 1 million audio recordings of customer service calls. The drives were in a network closet in a building recently vacated by BCBST. The servers in the closet were scheduled to be moved the following month. BCBST's investigation found that the records of over 1 million plan members were stored on the missing drives.

PENALTY – $ 1.5 million

INCIDENT – Hospice of North Idaho – lost laptop

The Hospice of North Idaho (HONI) reported the theft of an unencrypted laptop computer, containing records of 441 individuals. HIPAA requires that the confidentiality of PHI be maintained for 50 years after a person's death.

The OCR investigation found that HONI had not conducted an accurate and thorough Security Risk Analysis, and did not implement adequate security measures.

PENALTY - $ 50,000

LESSONS

- **ENCRYPT ALL DEVICES THAT MIGHT STORE PHI**

- **The time you must prove a device was encrypted is after it has been lost or stolen. There are IT management tools that will track encryption and document that it is installed and working. Have your IT department or IT vendor implement a reporting tool that will provide evidence to support your decision not to report a lost or stolen device, because it was encrypted.**

- **Use FIPS-140 certified encryption tools. By using encryption that meets this government standard, you should be able to defend against any questions about the quality of your encryption**

We have helped many types of Covered Entities and Business Associates build compliance programs and protect themselves by following our checklists for system deployments and retirements, and to check their systems to ensure that all devices that store PHI are properly encrypted.

Want to avoid a data breach? Want to validate that your compliance efforts are working? Not sure if your staff really "has HIPAA handled"?

Visit www.semelconsulting.com and use the Contact link.

Will Insurance Save You? Is Insurance an Alternative to Investing in Compliance?

You must have insurance, but it is not a substitute for a robust compliance program. And, it might not pay off just when you need it most.

Business insurance used to be limited to property and casualty coverage, and professional liability/malpractice insurance. In recent years, cyber liability insurance, and data breach insurance, have been added to the list of coverages available to businesses.

Cyber liability coverage includes the cost of attorneys to represent you, forensic and cyber security consulting, identity theft protection services, and settlements with victims.

Cyber liability coverage is new and does not have the history behind it for insurers to know their risks. Contrast it with life insurance, which is based on hundreds of years of data, with large numbers of claims for insurance companies to base their rates and their coverage limits.

Limitations in cyber liability policies make coverage different than malpractice insurance, which assumes a licensed professional like a doctor or lawyer makes a mistake. Cyber liability claims may be denied if you made a mistake on your insurance application, or by implementing the security controls you told the insurer you had in place.

How much coverage should you buy? Do you think $ 1 million in coverage sounds like a lot? Many organizations are underinsured, based on the costs from data breaches.

Do you go by the average case resolution penalty, since 2012, from the OCR - $ **1.5 million**?

Or, do you calculate the number of medical records you have times the cost-per-record in the annual Cost of a Data Breach Report, which for healthcare in 2016 was $ 402? According to that report, insurance only reduced the cost of a data breach by $ 8.60, bringing the cost per record to $ 391.

> $ 391 x **10,000 records** = $ **3.91 million**
>
> $ 391 x **25,000 records** = $ **9.8 million** (we see many small medical practices at this level)
>
> $ 391 x **100,000 records** = $ **39.1 million**

Or, do you look at the combination of penalties assessed against Triple-S Salud, a Puerto Rican health plan, that paid $ 6.8 million to the Puerto Rican insurance commissioner and another $ 3.5 million to the OCR, totaling $ 10.3 million?

Legal fees alone can easily exceed $ 100,000.

You may be liable for a breach caused by a Business Associate. Or, your Business Associate may not have enough liability coverage to cover the costs of a breach, leaving you on the hook.

INCIDENT – Cottage Health System – IT vendor published patient records to the Internet

Cottage Health paid an IT company to install a server. The server was accidently published to the Internet, exposing over 32,000 patient records to Google.

A class-action lawsuit was brought against Cottage Health and its IT company. Because its IT company did not have insurance, nor the financial ability to defend itself, Cottage Health contacted its insurance carrier, Columbia Casualty, and asked for legal representation and financial protection.

Columbia Casualty responded, provided legal representation, and settled the lawsuit for $ 4.1 million, while 'reserving its rights' to continue to investigate the incident.

During its investigation, Columbia Casualty discovered discrepancies between what Cottage Health said on its application it did to secure data, and what it was really doing.

Columbia Casualty sued Cottage Health to get the $ 4.1 million back, saying, "Cottage's application for coverage under the Columbia Policy contained misrepresentations and/or omissions of material fact that were made negligently or with intent to deceive concerning Cottage's data breach risk controls."

In other words, it did not matter if Cottage Health was mistaken, or was lying, when it misrepresented the facts on its application. The lawsuit further claimed that the data breach "was caused by Cottage's failure to maintain the risk controls identified in its application."

PENALTY – Sued by its insurance company for $ 4.1 million

Resolution: The lawsuit was thrown out by a judge because Columbia Casualty had not first attempted arbitration to settle the dispute, as required in its policy.

LESSONS

- **Buy Professional Liability/Errors & Omissions/Malpractice insurance**

- **Buy enough to meet your tolerance for risk, based on data breach costs and penalties**

- **Buy enough to satisfy requirements of your partners and clients**

- **Don't expect insurance to be a substitute for a robust security and compliance program**

- **Make sure your insurance agent understands your business**

- **Clarify the wording in your policy to make sure it covers all the services you offer**

- **Periodically review your insurance application and audit yourself for compliance. Ask your IT department or IT vendor for evidence proving everything is working as stated on your insurance application. If something isn't working, or got missed, fix the problem so your insurance company doesn't find a reason to deny a claim.**

We have helped many types of Covered Entities and Business Associates build compliance programs and validate that they are meeting the requirements of their cyber liability insurance policies.

Want to avoid a data breach? Want to validate that your compliance efforts are working? Not sure if your staff really "has HIPAA handled"?

Visit www.semelconsulting.com and use the Contact link.

Regulation Through Litigation

It's logical to think of HIPAA enforcement coming from the government officials tasked with regulatory compliance. But, your biggest threat may come from the attorney down the street. You know, the one on TV and all over billboards telling patients to sue their doctors.

Malpractice

HIPAA has been used successfully in a malpractice case. A jury determined that HIPAA is a Standard of Care, and that the pharmacist that violated a customer's rights should have followed the rules because everyone in healthcare knows about confidentiality and compliance.

Contractual Requirements

Many Covered Entities and Business Associates sign contracts and Data Use Agreements. Not complying, with or without a data breach, can result in a Breach of Contract lawsuit. Even without a suit, you may lose a relationship that is critical to your organization, and must return any money you collected.

Notice of Privacy Practices

A patient sued her doctor for Breach of Contract, saying the breach caused by the doctor was a breach of the Notice of Privacy Practices (NPP) she received when she became a patient. A Connecticut court agreed that the NPP was a contract, and that HIPAA is a Standard of Care that all healthcare providers should know and not violate.

Attorneys are going to conferences to learn how to litigate data breach claims. Cases can be brought against health care providers and health plans by patients and health plan members. Cases are also being brought against vendors and service providers by their clients, whose protected data has been breached by the vendor.

Here are a few of the topics that were discussed at a recent event:

-Class action and non-class action litigation

-Case valuation methods

-Settlement structures

-How relief is being defined

-Evolution of Damages Theories

-Strategies for Litigation

Cases have been dismissed when plaintiffs have not been able to prove that they were harmed by the release of their medical information. Others have been settled for millions of dollars. Many settlement details are kept secret so it is impossible to know what happened.

INCIDENT – Wellpoint

In 2010, Wellpoint, a parent company of multiple health plans, <u>was made aware of a HIPAA data breach when it was sued by an applicant</u> who discovered she could access the records of other health plan members.

INCIDENT – Walgreen's – Malpractice Lawsuit based on HIPAA Violation

Abigail Hinchy, Walgreen's customer, had a child fathered by her ex-boyfriend, Davion Peterson.

Peterson then informed his new girlfriend, Audra Withers, a Walgreens' pharmacist, that he was the father of Hinchy's child, and that he had contracted a sexually transmitted disease, which he may have passed on to her.

Hinchy received harassing text messages from her ex-boyfriend, Peterson, saying he had a printout of her prescriptions and accused her of being negligent with birth control, resulting in her becoming pregnant with his child. Peterson berated Hinchy for "getting pregnant on purpose" and threatened to release details of her prescription usage to her family unless she abandoned her paternity suit.

Through an Internet search, Hinchy discovered that Peterson had married Withers, the pharmacist.

Hinchy complained to Walgreens that she believed her pharmacy history had been accessed by Withers and given to her ex-boyfriend. Walgreens investigated, gave Withers a written warning, and required her to retake a HIPAA training course.

Hinchy sued Walgreens and Withers, alleging malpractice, invasion of privacy, and public disclosure of private facts.

Hinchy's claim against just Walgreens was for negligent training, negligent supervision, negligent retention, and negligence/professional malpractice. The judge threw out the charge of negligent training during the trial.

Jury Verdict - $ 1.8 million – 80% ($ 1.44 million) against Walgreens and Withers for Malpractice, and 20% against Peterson (the ex-boyfriend)

INCIDENT - Byrne vs. Avery Center for Obstetrics & Gynecology, PC - Breach of Contract lawsuit

Emily Byrne sued her OB/GYN clinic, Avery Center for Obstetrics & Gynecology, PC, for Negligence and Breach of Contract, after the clinic sent her medical records, without her authorization, to the attorney for her ex-boyfriend, who was suing her for paternity and visitation rights for the child he fathered.

From court documents:

> Before July 12, 2005, the (OB/GYN clinic) provided (Ms. Byrne) [with] gynecological and obstetrical care and treatment. The (OB/GYN clinic) provided its patients, including (Ms. Byrne), with notice of its privacy policy regarding protected health information and agreed, based on this policy and on law, that it would not disclose (Ms. Byrne)'s health information without her authorization.

> In May, 2004, (Ms. Byrne) began a personal relationship with Andro Mendoza, which lasted until September, 2004. . .

> In October, 2004, she instructed the (OB/GYN clinic) not to release her medical records to Mendoza. In March, 2005, she moved from Connecticut to Vermont where she presently lives.

> On May 31, 2005, Mendoza filed paternity actions against (Ms. Byrne) in Connecticut and Vermont. Thereafter, the (OB/GYN clinic) was served with a subpoena requesting its presence together with (Ms. Byrne)'s medical records at the New Haven Regional Children's [Probate Court] on July 12, 2005.

> The (OB/GYN clinic) did not alert (Ms. Byrne) of the subpoena, file a motion to quash it or appear in court. Rather, the (OB/GYN clinic) mailed a copy of (Ms. Byrne)'s medical file to the court around July 12, 2005. In September, 2005, '[Mendoza] informed (Ms. Byrne) by telephone that he reviewed (Ms. Byrne)'s medical file in the court file.'

On September 15, 2005, (Ms. Byrne) filed a motion to seal her medical file, which was granted. (Ms. Byrne) alleges that she suffered harassment and extortion threats from Mendoza since he viewed her medical records.

...Mendoza has utilized the information contained within (Ms. Byrne's) records to file numerous civil actions, including paternity and visitation actions, against (Ms. Byrne), her attorney, her father and her father's employer, and to threaten her with criminal charges....

Verdict/Settlement – Still going through the judicial process

INCIDENT - Cottage Health System - Insurance company sued its customer to recover $ 4.1 million

Cottage Health used its insurance coverage to receive legal representation and settle a $ 4.125 million class action suit with its patients.

In a lawsuit complaint filed by its insurer, Columbia Casualty, to recover legal fees and the $ 4.125 million, the insurance company stated that Cottage Health's insurance application "contained misrepresentations and/or omissions of material fact that were made negligently or with intent to deceive concerning Cottage's data breach risk controls."

In other words, it did not matter whether Cottage Health intentionally lied to its insurer on the application, or if the incorrect information was just a mistake, Columbia Casualty wanted its millions back.

Resolution: The lawsuit was thrown out by a judge because Columbia Casualty had not first attempted arbitration to settle the dispute, as required in its policy.

LESSONS –

- Don't think your biggest threat is the federal government catching you in a HIPAA violation. Your biggest threat may be the attorney representing a patient, or representing your insurance company

- A Notice of Privacy Practices was validated by a court to be a contract with a patient, in a Breach of Contract lawsuit

- HIPAA was approved as a Standard of Care in a Malpractice lawsuit

- You should consider your disciplinary process for employees who violate HIPAA. Just writing someone up after a breach, and require additional HIPAA training, may make you lose a lawsuit

- Breaching a patient's confidential information can result in financial and personal harm

- Attorneys are being trained on how to bring lawsuits after confidentiality and data breaches

- When you receive a subpoena, you should not respond without getting advice from your attorney

- Your attorney should understand HIPAA. If you are a Covered Entity, and you are sharing PHI with your attorney, your attorney is a Business Associate, and must sign your Business Associate Agreement and implement a HIPAA compliance program

---

We are not attorneys, but have been introduced to clients by their attorneys who trust us to provide compliance and cyber security advice.

Want to avoid a data breach? Want to validate that your compliance efforts are working? Not sure if your staff really "has HIPAA handled"?

Visit www.semelconsulting.com and use the Contact link.

Why Aren't HIPAA Security Basics No-Brainers?

HIPAA has been the law since 2003. The Security Rule protecting data came into effect in 2005. Even if an organization did not get to all of the items in the Security Rule, why are so many missing the first four?

The foundation of a HIPAA security program are the first four items in the HIPAA Security Rule, which have been required for HIPAA Covered Entities since 2005, and HIPAA Business Associates since 2013.

1. Conduct a **Security Risk Analysis** identifying the locations of your data, and what vulnerabilities and threats can affect its security. 45 CFR 164.308(a)(1)

2. Implement a **Risk Management** program to address the risks identified in your Risk Analysis.

3. Adopt a **Sanction Policy** describing what will happen to workforce members who violate the regulations, and communicate the information to your staff.

4. Conduct periodic **Information System Activity Reviews** – analyze logs or reports of activity in your network, databases, and firewalls, to identify unusual or unauthorized activity.

More than half of the multi-million dollar HIPAA penalties cite a missing or inadequate risk analysis as an underlying cause of the breach.

A risk analysis is at the top of the list in the HIPAA Security Rule, and one of the few items identified as being required to respond to a HIPAA audit.

Why do so many penalties against companies that conducted risk analyses, cite their lack of risk management as an underlying cause?

Why have so many organizations failed to implement a set of HIPAA IT policies to comply with the Security Rule, communicate the policies they have adopted, and trained their workforce members?

Why do so many organizations fail to monitor the activity in their networks, fail to log access to PHI, and to review the logs to identify unusual or unauthorized activity?

WHY HAVE SO MANY ORGANIZATIONS FAILED TO ENCRYPT THEIR DATA, when encrypted data is exempt from breach reporting if a device is lost or stolen?

More than half of the multimillion HIPAA penalties were for the loss of unencrypted devices.

If the data had been encrypted, the loss of the device would not have been reportable.

WHY DO SO MANY HEALTHCARE PROFESSIONALS SNOOP in patient records, when HIPAA's Minimum Necessary Access requirement says they may only look at a record for business purposes?

WHY DO SO MANY HEALTHCARE ORGANIZATIONS FAIL TO SIGN BUSINESS ASSOCIATE AGREEMENTS WITH THEIR VENDORS?

INCIDENT – Advocate Health System – stolen computers, Business Associate hacked, laptop stolen from employee's car

In July, 2013, four **unencrypted** laptops were stolen from a suburban Chicago office. Later in the summer, one of its Business Associates was accessed by an unauthorized user. Finally, in November, Advocate reported yet another theft of an **unencrypted** laptop computer, from an employee's car. What was remarkable about these breaches was that 4 million patient records were breached.

PENALTY - $ 5.5 million

INCIDENT – Feinstein Institute for Medical Research – unencrypted laptop stolen from employee's car

OCR's investigation found the **unencrypted** laptop included approximately 13,000 names of research participants, dates of birth, addresses, social security numbers, diagnoses, laboratory results, medications, and medical information relating to potential participation in a research study.

PENALTY - $ 3.9 million

INCIDENT – State of Alaska Department of Health & Social Services – lost unencrypted hard drive

An **unencrypted** hard drive used by the State of Alaska Department of Health & Social Services' IT staff was stolen from an employee's car (starting to see a pattern here?)

PENALTY - $ 1.7 million (taxpayer funds, almost $ 2 per Alaska resident)

INCIDENT – South Broward Hospital d/b/a Memorial Health System – impermissible access to PHI

In 2012, Memorial Health System reported that two employees inappropriately accessed patient information. During its internal investigation, the health system discovered additional unauthorized access by 12 other employees. This led to federal criminal charges of selling PHI and filing fraudulent tax returns with the IRS.

The OCR investigation found that 80,000 patient records had been accessed by a former employee, whose employment had been terminated, but who still had access to the health record system.

According to government records, the health system also "failed to implement procedures to regularly review records of information system activity, such as audit logs, access reports, and security incident tracking reports," all required by HIPAA.

PENALTY - $ 5.5 million

INCIDENT – Raleigh Orthopaedic Clinic – shared PHI with a vendor without a Business Associate Agreement

Raleigh Orthopaedic Clinic probably thought the deal was too good to be true. A company offered to scan its x-ray films into digital files, for free, in exchange for harvesting the silver from the x-ray films. PHI belonging to 17,300 patients was breached, because the orthopaedic clinic shared the x-rays with the vendor, but had not signed a HIPAA Business Associate Agreement.

PENALTY - $ 750,000

LESSONS

- **ENCRYPT. ENCRYPT. ENCRYPT.**

- **Don't delay encrypting your devices**

In an interview with HealthcareInfoSecurity.com, Thor Ryan, State of Alaska Department of Health & Social Services' Chief Security Officer, said "Be proactive. The steps you're working on now or planning to do to improve compliance, do that expediently. We were more than halfway through our encryption project when an unencrypted hard drive was stolen. With the benefit of hindsight, we could have saved millions of dollars."

- **Implement a Domain Network, so you can log access to files containing PHI**

- **Turn on activity logging on your servers, your firewalls, and your databases**

- **Review the logs for unusual and unauthorized activity**

- **Unless you are a very small organization, you will need to implement a log management tool to review and sort your logs**

- **Retain your logs for 6 years, and have them available for an audit or data breach investigation**

- **Sign Business Associate Agreements with ALL vendors and partners who may come in contact with your PHI**

- **Make sure your Business Associates have signed Business Associate Agreements with ALL of their subcontractors and vendors who may come in contact with your PHI.**

- **Guidance issued in 2016 makes it clear that cloud service providers and data centers are Business Associates, even if they do not access your PHI**

- Guidance issued in 2016 states that a ransomware attack is a HIPAA data breach. Do whatever you can to prevent your employees from clicking on a phishing email that could trigger an attack

- To comply with HIPAA, you either need a qualified full-time IT staff, or Managed Services from a qualified, and HIPAA-compliant, IT vendor

We love working with MSPs who introduce us to their clients. We do not sell IT products or services.

Want to avoid a data breach? Want to validate that your compliance efforts are working? Not sure if your staff really "has HIPAA handled"?

Visit **www.semelconsulting.com** and use the **Contact link.**

Skilled Nursing & Home Health Care

It is hard enough to implement patient confidentiality in doctor's offices and hospitals, where patients visit for a short time. Skilled Nursing and Home Health Care organizations face a bigger challenge, because of the long-term relationships that develop between patients, caregivers, and families. I know, because I'm one of them.

Skilled nursing facilities and home health care organizations have serious challenges to complying with HIPAA and other confidentiality requirements.

I was the Chief Information Officer for a hospital with a 120-bed skilled nursing facility, and a home health care service, and have conducted HIPAA Security Risk Analyses and HIPAA compliance assessments for many skilled nursing facilities and home health care organizations. I am the health care proxy for my mom, who is in an assisted living facility, and I have had other relatives and friends in skilled nursing facilities.

Many of the skilled nursing facilities and home health care organizations we have worked with have done little to comply. Some are owned by government agencies, with others owned by corporations whose executives are not familiar with the compliance requirements. Many simply don't know what they don't know. Some are challenged by languages. We have worked with facilities with residents and staff that primarily speak Spanish, Korean, and Russian.

There is a lot of guidance about HIPAA regulations for doctor's offices, clinics, and hospitals. Large health care organizations have compliance specialists on staff. Doctors and nurses are trained about confidentiality for years while in school, and with ongoing training through their employers.

Patients usually stay in acute care hospital beds for just a few days. They, and their families, rarely strike up friendships with other patients. They, and their families, don't build relationships with staff members.

Contrast that with skilled nursing facilities. They are the long-term home for their residents. Those in for rehab after an injury or surgery often stay for weeks or months.

The residents and patients live with each other, become friends, eat together, attend social activities, and are often aware when someone becomes ill or if a room suddenly is empty. Family members get to know the residents, their families, and the staff. (When I take my mom out for dinner I know what goodies to bring back to the nursing staff.)

In the acute care side of the hospital where I was the CIO, we had a high number of nurses and doctors, with very few aides helping with patients. The skilled nursing facility, and our home health care department, were the opposite of the hospital, with most of the staff made up of Certified Nursing Assistants (CNA), who took a 12-week course that included only a small amount of confidentiality training.

CNA's have been surprised when we tell them that they can not only be fired, but can lose their licenses, and their careers, if they violate a resident or patient's confidentiality.

Home health care faces additional challenges because patients are treated at home, requiring the health care staff to constantly transfer paper and electronic medical records. While hospitals and skilled nursing facilities have secure networks and online health record systems, home health care aides and nurses rely on paper and portable devices, because they cannot expect an Internet connection at a patient's home.

INCIDENT – Skilled Nursing Facility – CNA posted deceased resident's medical info on social media

In the middle of one of our compliance assessments at a skilled nursing facility, the director called me to say that one of his CNA's had posted information about a resident on her Facebook account, a violation of their corporate policies.

The facility director went on to say that the resident had died, and the CNA listed the medical complications leading up to his death. He was reading everything to me from Facebook. Before we went any further, I asked the director to take a screen-shot of his computer, so we had the evidence, but then to hang up on me and get the CNA to remove the post from her social media account.

While it is common to assume that everyone in a skilled nursing facility is old, I had met the resident during my site visit. He was in his 50's, had been severely injured in an accident, and was physically deformed. The resident was hospitalized for a critical medical condition, and decided to end his hospital treatment and return to the skilled nursing facility, to pass away in peace. All of this had been in the CNA's Facebook post.

The CNA was disciplined. She explained that she knew she shouldn't have posted information about a resident on social media, but she thought it was OK because the resident had died. She thought his HIPAA rights died with him.

The director called me later to inform me that a friend of the deceased resident had threatened to sue the skilled nursing facility for wrongful death. She said she could have talked the resident out of dying if the facility had just called her to intervene (which would have been another HIPAA violation.)

INCIDENT – Skilled Nursing Facility – sharing information about a resident being hidden in a facility

I received a call from another facility director informing me that one of his CNA's had 'outed' a disabled resident being hidden in his facility from someone who had sexually molested her.

The CNA was related to the alleged molester, and had called him to say that his victim had just moved into the skilled nursing facility.

I asked the director if he had called the police, and he said he hadn't because he was worried about HIPAA. I explained that HIPAA allowed for this type of information sharing, and asked him to call law enforcement to request protection for his resident.

The CNA was fired. The resident was moved elsewhere.

INCIDENT – Resident transferred from skilled nursing facility, sought as a missing person

I received a call from an executive of a medical transport company, saying that her company had transferred a skilled nursing facility resident, and that she had just seen a news report that the man's family was looking for him and had engaged the police in a missing person search.

She was upset that HIPAA was preventing her from notifying the police of the man's whereabouts.

I led her to the federal website that lists circumstances when a health care professional can communicate someone's location to law enforcement. It is not a HIPAA violation to inform law enforcement about the location of a fugitive, or the subject of a missing person case.

LESSON –

- Skilled nursing facility resident information or pictures should never be published on social media, in advertising, or in a facility, without proper signed HIPAA authorizations

- HIPAA privacy rights extend for 50 years from the time of death. After a death, the personal representative for the decedent's estate takes over responsibility for HIPAA requests

- It is permissible to share information with law enforcement when someone's safety is at stake, if you know the location of a fugitive, or of a missing person being sought by law enforcement

We understand the unique HIPAA challenges faced in skilled nursing and home health care.

Want to avoid a data breach? Want to validate that your compliance efforts are working? Not sure if your staff really "has HIPAA handled"?

Visit www.semelconsulting.com and use the Contact link.

Should You Do Your Own Security Risk Analysis?

You've seen the ads.

FREE RISK ANALYSIS!

DO YOUR OWN RISK ANALYSIS IN 15 MINUTES!

Complete our Online Questionnaire and we will send you your Risk Score!

Subscribe to our Online Portal for all your HIPAA compliance needs!

Conducting a risk analysis is just like a doctor conducting an accurate and thorough physical. Would you trust a physical if it was free? Would you trust a physical conducted by yourself in just 15 minutes? Would you trust a physical done by your doctor just asking you questions? Would you trust your health to a doctor who just had you store your medical information in a cloud service, and then called to discuss the information?

The first item in the HIPAA Security Rule is a Security Risk Analysis, an assessment to identify the vulnerabilities and threats that can affect the security of your electronic data. This is the most important step in the HIPAA Security process, because it is the foundation to the processes you will implement to protect your data.

If you get the Security Risk Analysis right, you will protect your organization, your patients or customers, and your career. If you get it wrong, then every step you take will be wrong.

The federal government offers tools for smaller organizations to use to complete their risk analysis. You see ads from companies offering free 5-minute risk assessments and automated questionnaires that will determine your risk score. The problem with all of these is that they assume you know the right answers to the questions.

I have been doing assessments for 14 years and have never encountered a situation where everything was as we were told.

We have discovered

- data in many places that supposedly had no data

- enabled network users whose employment had been terminated

- data backups weren't happening

- systems were not receiving security patches and updates

- anti-virus protection was not installed on every device

- that users were storing data in the cloud

- retired servers were still connected to the network

- passwords set to never expire

- generic usernames shared by multiple users

- passwords taped to displays

- firewalls that were running but not protecting networks

- missing Business Associate Agreements

- and a lot more

For each item listed I was told by our clients that everything was just fine. If they had used one of the automated tools, or simply answered a questionnaire, they would have received a great risk score and thought that they were protected. In fact, one of the biggest risks to their data was that they believed they were OK.

We have also seen Security Risk Analyses conducted by organization staff that failed to document obvious security and compliance issues. Management was unaware of their risks until we shared our reports with them.

In April, 2014, the FBI warned healthcare organizations that, "The biggest vulnerability (to the security of protected health data) was the perception of IT health care professionals' beliefs that their current perimeter defenses and compliance strategies were working when clearly the data states otherwise."

In December, 2015, the FBI informed two hospitals that their patient data was for sale on the Internet. One may have been compromised for more than three years.

INCIDENT – Hollywood Presbyterian Hospital

In February, 2016, Hollywood Presbyterian Hospital was hit by a devastating ransomware attack that encrypted all its computers, with a ransom demand for the key to unlock the data.

The hospital was down for 10 days, causing it to transfer patients and discontinue services. Their communications systems were down, meaning they could not use e-mails to communicate, or send prescriptions to pharmacies. They had to resort to paper faxes, handwritten notes, and handwritten medical records.

Management portrayed themselves as helpless victims, even though it became obvious that they had never developed plans or implemented systems to prevent, respond to, or recover from, a ransomware attack.

After this incident, the OCR issued guidance stating that ransomware attacks are HIPAA breaches under the HITECH Act.

PENALTY – Paid $ 17,000 ransom to gain access to its data

> **I expect a financial penalty based on the OCR's guidance, and the negative publicity against the hospital because it lost its ability to treat patients. It seems obvious that the hospital did not conduct an accurate and thorough risk analysis, and implement risk management strategies, like a robust backup system, or else it would have been better prepared for the ransomware attack.**

INCIDENT – St. Joseph Health System

St. Joseph's Health System made PHI available to Google and other search engines. 31,800 individuals were affected. The files contained patient names, BMI, blood pressure, lab results, smoking status, diagnoses lists, medication allergies, advance directive status, and demographic information (language, ethnicity, race, sex, and birth date).

When it implemented the new system that accidently connected the data to the Internet, St. Joseph's should have conducted a Security Risk Analysis to identify the risks associated with the new system.

PENALTY - $ 2.14 million

ASSESSMENT FINDING – Anonymous Client – Business Associate – No offsite backup

I was doing an assessment for a Business Associate and was attempting to find out how the PHI they stored was being backed up, a HIPAA requirement.

Their IT vendor had not provided the information, and was unreachable. I asked the bookkeeper to pull the payment file for the IT vendor so I could see the type of backup they were paying for. An offsite backup service was listed, at a fee of $ 700 per month. They had been paying for the service for six months.

I went through the server and the local computers, and could not find the software required for the backup service listed on the invoice. Nor could I find any other backup utility running.

The client called the IT vendor, who sent a technician to the office. He looked at all the computers and then said, "I can't explain it, but we have been charging you for backup services that we never installed."

For six months the client had been paying $ 700 per month for backup services they weren't receiving. Worse, their data had not been backed up, meaning that a system failure or burglary could have resulted in them losing critical data, forever.

PENALTY – The IT company was fired by the client

ASSESSMENT FINDING – Anonymous Client – Business Associate – Not Complying With Contract

Prior to our assessments, we ask to see any contracts our client may have signed that include cyber security or compliance requirements. The clients are sometimes shocked when they look at contracts they have filed away, without implementing procedures to comply with cyber security controls that are written into the contracts.

During an assessment of a Business Associate, I asked them what health care systems they worked with. They listed some of the most well-known health care systems in the country. When they mentioned one of them, I asked them to bring me the Business Associate Agreement they had signed.

Our client brought it to me, and I showed her the 4-page cyber security requirements and started reading them out loud. As I read each one, I asked what her company had done to comply with her contract. None of the items was required in a Business Associate Agreement, but this health care organization had tacked it onto the Business Associate Agreement they had everyone sign.

Our client was shocked that she had filed away a contract without knowing it had 4 pages of specific requirements she had to follow.

We shifted our compliance program from focusing just on HIPAA to including their contractual obligations.

PENALTY – None, but it was possible the health care system could have sued them for breach of contract if there was a data breach. They could have also lost their relationship with the health care system if they were audited and found to be non-compliant with their contract.

LESSONS –

- Outsource your risk analysis to professionals who have skills, years of experience, and the tools required to conduct an accurate and thorough analysis

- If you are a non-technical decision-maker, make sure you review the risk analysis with someone who can explain the technical findings and guide you to allocate the resources required to reduce your risks

- Require reports and demonstrations to prove that your systems and processes are working

- Require evidence of an actual test-restore of your data, or your entire functions, from your backups. Seeing a 'backup has completed' message is not proof that your critical functions can be recovered in an emergency

- Implement a multi-stage approach to preventing a ransomware attack, including employee training to prevent phishing message attacks; firewalls and anti-malware protection; blacklisting and whitelisting, and having quickly-accessible backups to reload if your data is encrypted

- HIPAA may be only one of your compliance requirements. Make sure you work with an expert who can guide you through federal and state laws, industry regulations, contractual obligations, and insurance policy requirements.

We have 14 years' experience conducting accurate and thorough Security Risk Analyses and compliance assessments. We use 'under the skin' tools to validate technical security. We are certified in compliance and can help with federal and state laws, industry regulations, contractual obligations, and insurance policy requirements.

Want to avoid a data breach? Want to validate that your compliance efforts are working? Not sure if your staff really "has HIPAA handled"?

Visit www.semelconsulting.com and use the Contact link.

Endorsements & Accolades

"Mike Semel has a unique ability to take a complex regulation like HIPAA and make it simple. While Mike has always been great at helping people remedy their HIPAA headaches, I'm even more excited that Mike's expertise in this book will help people avoid the HIPAA problems in the first place.

A little bit of HIPAA compliance work now is worth the effort to avoid the millions of dollars and shame of a HIPAA breach and fine later. Some might argue that HIPAA and headaches go together like peas and carrots. That's often the state of Mike's clients before they started working with him."

John Lynn, Editor & Publisher,
Healthcare Scene/EMR & HIPAA

"I am refreshed with Mike Semel's approach, which is to use a practical application of his HIPAA and cloud knowledge to protect our business, along with our clients and their patients. When I started our innovative cloud platform for healthcare, I thought HIPAA was a basic compliance requirement. Mike showed me that compliance is critical to protecting our brand."

Paul Magelli, CEO, Apervita

"This is a must read for anyone who is touched by HIPAA compliance concerns, which, in reality, is most of us!

Mike Semel is a forward looking Go Giver who is always looking for ways to help people avoid the pitfalls of HIPAA with education and great ideas. He's on the cutting edge of understanding the law, and more importantly how to apply it for the benefit of customers and those who take care of them."

Arlin Sorensen, Founder, HTG Peer Groups

"Mike Semel has been an invaluable HIPAA mentor to thousands of IT experts who are part of The ASCII Group, the largest and oldest group of Managed IT Service Providers in the world. We rely on Mike to help our members with the ins and outs of HIPAA."

Alan D. Weinberger. Chairman and CEO, The ASCII Group

"Mike Semel's technical experience and compliance expertise free me up to concentrate on the legal issues affecting this highly complex area of health care law. Mike is a HIPAA/HITECH resource that I could not do without in the effective representation of my clients!"

E. Michael Flanagan. Healthcare Attorney

About the Author

Mike Semel owns Semel Consulting, and is certified on HIPAA (and other regulatory) compliance; cyber security; and Business Continuity planning. He has owned or managed technology companies for over 30 years; served as Chief Information Officer (CIO) for a hospital and a K-12 school district; and managed operations at an online backup company.

Mike chaired CompTIA's IT Security Community, helped develop CompTIA's Security Trustmark Plus, and is an active member of the FBI's Infragard program. Mike has authored HIPAA training courses, and has had numerous articles published in magazines and on websites. He has spoken at NASA, the New York State Cyber Security Conference, and many healthcare and IT conferences.

He has managed hundreds of HIPAA and regulatory compliance assessments, and Meaningful Use Security Risk Analyses, for doctors, hospitals, labs, nursing homes, home health care agencies, government agencies, and Business Associates. Mike has created Business Continuity plans for small businesses, healthcare organizations, and financial institutions. His business continuity plans meet regulatory requirements and have helped businesses survive the Joplin tornado, Hurricane Irene, SuperStorm Sandy, and many smaller disruptions you never heard of.

Mike has been an Emergency Medical Technician; fire department rescue captain; was Safety Director at the Watkins Glen International auto race track, and traveled with the IndyCar Safety Team for 19 years.

Made in the USA
Columbia, SC
12 January 2019